This little cook book is dedicated to you who would like to give your families more of your homemade good things, if you only had the time.

Bisquick makes that possible ... good homemade food, quickly prepared. You can cook with love and enjoy the cooking more, when you use this cook book and your Bisquick. Once you start, I know you'll want to try every idea in the book.

Betty Crocker

Biscuits: *How to make them perfect*

Heat oven to 450° (hot). Add ⅔ cup milk all at once to 2 cups Bisquick. Stir with fork into a soft dough. Beat dough vigorously 20 strokes, until stiff and slightly sticky.

Roll dough around on cloth-covered board lightly dusted with Bisquick to prevent sticking.

Betty Crocker

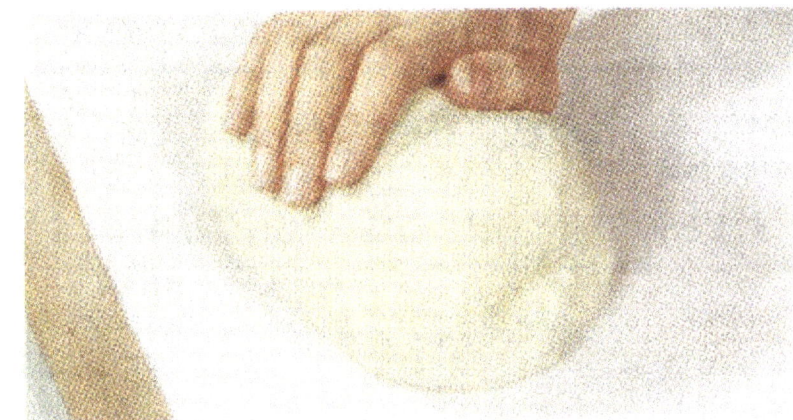

Knead gently 8 to 10 times to smooth up dough.

Roll ½" thick. Biscuits double in size in baking. Dip cutter in Bisquick. Cut close together to save rerolling.

Bake on ungreased shiny baking sheet *10 to 15 min.*; close together for soft sides, 1" apart for crusty sides. *Makes 12 2" biscuits.*

For Drop Biscuits ... drop dough with spoon on greased baking sheet. Bake as above.

For Richer Biscuits ... follow directions above—except mix ¼ cup soft butter or shortening, or 3 tbsp. cooking (salad) oil into Bisquick before mixing in milk.

For Buttermilk Biscuits ... use ¾ cup buttermilk for liquid. It may be necessary to use a few additional tablespoons of buttermilk to make a dough of soft consistency.

Dress up your biscuits 10 ways

Kind	Add to recipe	Serve with
Bacon	⅓ cup crisply cooked diced bacon	grapefruit, scrambled eggs
Cheese	½ cup grated sharp cheese	veal steak and vegetables
Chives	¼ cup finely chopped chives	wieners and baked beans
Curry	¼ tsp. curry powder	chicken casserole fruit salad
Ham	½ cup chopped boiled or baked ham	cheese soufflé, green salad
Herb	¼ tsp. nutmeg, ½ tsp. crumbled dry sage, and 1¼ tsp. caraway seeds	beef or veal stew
Lemon	1 tsp. grated lemon rind. Add 2 tbsp. lemon juice to ½ cup milk and use for milk in directions.	crispy fried fish
Olive	¼ cup chopped stuffed olives	sea food or meat casserole
Peanut	⅓ cup chopped peanuts	pot roast and vegetables
Salami	½ cup chopped salami sausage	mixed vegetables and cheese salad

Pecan Rolls

Betty Crocker

Mix ½ cup *each* melted butter, brown sugar. Spoon into 12 large muffin cups with three pecan halves in each. Cover with Biscuit dough; bake 15 minutes. Quick and delicious for Sunday brunch.

Butter Sticks

Heat oven to 450° (hot). Make Rolled Biscuit dough (recipe page 3)—except add 2 tbsp. dry onion soup mix. Roll dough into a rectangle, 10×6″. Cut in half lengthwise. Cut each half into 12 strips (about 3×½″). Melt ⅓ cup butter and add 2 tbsp. dry onion soup mix; pour half of it into oblong pan, 13×9½×2″. Place strips in pan. Pour remaining butter over tops. *Bake 10 to 15 min.*

Quantity Biscuits

For 60 Medium. Serves 30.

10 cups Bisquick
(40-oz. pkg. or two 20-oz. pkg.)
3⅓ cups milk

For 100 Medium. Serves 50.

15 cups Bisquick (60-oz. pkg.)
5 cups milk

Follow Biscuit directions (page 3).

Main dishes *with biscuit topping*

Meat and Vegetable Pie

1 lb. stewing beef (cubed)
½ cup Bisquick
½ tsp. salt
⅛ tsp. pepper
⅛ tsp. paprika, if desired
1 medium tomato, chopped; or ½ cup canned tomatoes
1 to 2 small onions, chopped
2 large carrots, sliced
1 small clove garlic, cut up

¼ tsp. Worcestershire sauce
salt and pepper

Roll meat in mixture of Bisquick, salt, pepper, and paprika. Brown meat thoroughly on all sides in a little hot fat. Add tomatoes, onions, carrots, and garlic; sauté until onions are transparent. Add enough water to cover meat and vegetables. Cover tightly and cook over low heat until meat is tender, 1½ to 2 hr. Add Worcestershire sauce, salt, and pepper. *Heat oven to 425° (hot).* Pour stew in 1½-qt. baking dish and cover with ½ recipe for Biscuits (recipe [page 3](page_3)). Bake *about 12 min.* until biscuits are a golden brown. *2 to 3 servings.*

Chicken Pot Pie

¼ cup chicken fat or butter
¼ cup Bisquick
1½ tsp. salt
¼ tsp. pepper
2 cups chicken stock (saved from stewing chicken)
⅔ cup cream
3 to 4 cups chicken (cut in large pieces)

Heat oven to 450° (hot). Heat chicken fat. Blend in Bisquick, salt, pepper. Remove from heat. Stir in chicken stock, cream, chicken. Cook over low heat until thickened (about 5 min.). Pour *hot* filling into baking dish, 11½×7½×1½″. Cover with Richer Biscuit dough (recipe [page 3](page_3)) rolled out to fit top of baking dish. Cut 2 or 3 slits in center. Bake *about 15 min. 4 to 6 servings.*

Note: If desired, use chicken fat for shortening in Biscuit recipe.

Deep-Dish Salmon-Cheese Pie

1 tbsp. chopped onion

2 tbsp. butter or other fat
¼ cup Bisquick
1½ cups milk
1 cup grated sharp Cheddar cheese
1 lb. can salmon, drained and broken into large pieces
1 tsp. salt
few grains pepper

Heat oven to 450° (hot). Sauté onion in butter. Remove from heat. Blend in Bisquick. Slowly stir in milk. Bring to boil over low heat, stirring constantly. Boil 1 min. Stir in rest of ingredients. Turn hot mixture into greased 1½-qt. baking dish and heat in oven until mixture bubbles. Make ½ Biscuit dough (recipe page 3). Pat or roll out to fit top of baking dish. Place on hot mixture. Cut 2 or 3 slits in center. Bake *about 15 min.* or until topping is brown. *4 to 6 servings.*

Tuna Pinwheel Roll

two 7-oz. cans tuna, with 2 tbsp. oil
½ cup chopped onion
½ cup grated sharp cheese
¼ cup chopped parsley
1 tsp. celery salt
½ tsp. salt
¼ tsp. pepper
1 egg, slightly beaten

Heat oven to 375° (quick mod.). Mix all ingredients except set aside 2 tbsp. of egg. Make Biscuit dough (recipe page 3). Roll into a rectangle, 15×10". Spread with tuna filling. Roll like jelly roll, starting with wide side. Place on well greased baking sheet in ring shape, with seam side down. Pinch ends together. Slice 12 even slices almost to the center edge, leaving about 1". Turn each piece on its side to show filling. Brush all over with remaining egg. Bake *25 to 30 min.* Serve with Bleu Cheese Sauce: ½ cup Bleu cheese, crumbled, in 2 cups medium white sauce. *4 to 6 servings.*

Meat Turnovers

Heat oven to 450° (hot). Make Richer Biscuit dough (recipe [page 3](page_3)). Roll into rectangle, 18×10". Cut in 8 pieces, 5×4½". Place slice of cooked or canned meat on half of square. Spread with 1 tbsp. chili sauce or pickle relish. Fold dough over meat and seal edges with fork. Slit top. Bake about *15 min.* on greased baking sheet. *4 to 8 servings.*

Baked Meat Sandwich

1 lb. ground lean pork
½ cup chopped onion
¼ cup grated Parmesan cheese
½ cup grated Swiss cheese
1 large egg, beaten
¼ tsp. Tabasco sauce
1½ tsp. salt

2 tbsp. minced parsley

Heat oven to 400° (mod. hot). Cook pork and onion over low heat until no longer pink. (Do not brown. Stir with fork to break up as it cooks.) Cool. Mix in rest of ingredients. Add ¼ cup mayonnaise to Biscuit dough (recipe page 3). Mix well with fork. Spread half of dough in well greased square pan, 8×8×2″. Spread meat mixture over dough. Spread rest of dough over mixture. (The top will even out during baking.) Brush with beaten egg yolk to give crusty glaze. Bake *25 to 30 min.* Cut in slices about ½″ thick and serve hot or cold.

Saucy Pigs in Blankets

Heat oven to 450° (hot). Make Rolled Biscuit dough (recipe page 3). Roll into circle ⅛″ thick. Cut circle into 8 equal wedges. Spread each wedge with 1 tbsp. well drained sauerkraut. Roll a frankfurter in each wedge, starting at wide end and seal well by pinching tip into roll. Sprinkle rolls with poppy seeds. Place on baking sheet. Bake *about 15 min.* Serve immediately with hot tomato sauce and additional sauerkraut on the side. *Makes 8.*

Main Dish Shortcakes

(Use Richer Biscuit dough—page 3)

• *Plain Individual Shortcakes*

Roll dough about ¾″ thick, and cut with 3″ round cutter. Bake. Split and serve with desired filling.

• *Plain Large Shortcake*

Pat out ½ of dough in round or square 8″ pan, dot with butter. Pat out rest of dough and place on top. Bake. Split and serve with desired filling.

• *Large Shortcake in Ring*

Spread dough in well greased 8 or 9" ring mold. Bake. Turn out on large platter. Fill center with desired filling.

• *Creamed Meat or Sea Food*

Add to medium white sauce cut-up cooked chicken, turkey, veal, pork, ham, tuna, salmon, shrimp, crabmeat, or lobster.

• *Meat or Sea Food à la King*

To creamed meat or sea food, add sautéed mushrooms, sliced hard-cooked eggs, chopped pimientos, etc.

• *Curried Meat or Sea Food*

Add a little curry powder when making white sauce for creamed meat or sea food. Delicious with chicken, lamb, veal, shrimp. With it, offer several relishes, such as chopped salted peanuts, ground fresh coconut, chutney, sweet pickled onions, hard-cooked egg put through a sieve, chopped pickle, and chopped crisp bacon.

Oven-Crisp Chicken and Biscuits

1 cup Bisquick
2 tsp. salt
¼ tsp. pepper
2 tsp. paprika
½ cup shortening (half butter)
1 cut-up frying chicken

Heat oven to 425° (hot). Mix first four ingredients in paper bag. Place shortening in oblong pan, 13×9½×2" and set in oven to melt. Shake chicken in bag to coat thoroughly. Place chicken, skin-side-down, in single layer in hot shortening. Bake *45 min.*; then turn. Meanwhile, make Rolled Biscuit dough (recipe page_3). Roll dough ¼" thick and cut into biscuits. Push chicken to one side in pan; place biscuits in single layer on other side. Bake *another 15 min.*, or until biscuits are lightly browned and chicken tender. Place chicken and biscuits on serving platter. For gravy, add 2 tbsp. Bisquick (saved from dredgings) to drippings in pan. Bring to boil. Add 1½ cups hot water. Boil 1 min. *4 servings.*

Asparagus Shortcake with Cheese Sauce

Heat oven to 450° (hot). Make Biscuit dough (recipe page 3). Roll out ¼" thick. Cut into 4 or 5" rounds. Bake *about 10 min.* Split. Serve sandwich-fashion with about 5 spears of freshly cooked asparagus between biscuit halves. Make *Cheese Sauce* by heating 1½ cups medium white sauce, 2 cups grated sharp cheese (½ lb.), ¼ tsp. dry mustard, and few grains thyme over hot water until cheese melts. Pour over top. Garnish with sprig of parsley. *4 to 5 servings.*

Muffins or Coffee Cake

2 tbsp. sugar
1 egg
¾ cup milk
2 cups Bisquick

Heat oven to 400° (mod. hot). Blend ingredients together. Then beat vigorously 30 seconds.

Muffins: Fill well greased muffin pans ⅔ full. Bake *15 min. Makes 12.*

Coffee Cake: Spread into greased 9" round layer pan, or 8 or 9" square pan. Sprinkle with mixture of 2 tsp. cinnamon, ¼ cup sugar, 2 tbsp. Bisquick, 2 tbsp. soft butter. Blend with fork until crumbly. Bake *20 to 25 min.*

Dress up your muffins 4 ways

Kind	Add to recipe	Serve with
Bacon	Fold ¼ cup crisp, diced, cooked bacon into batter.	cottage cheese and fruit salad
Cheese	Add ½ to 1 cup grated, sharp, yellow cheese.	any meat casserole
Chive	Fold ¼ cup chopped chives into batter.	salmon loaf
Orange	Use ½ cup orange juice for ½ cup of the milk. Sprinkle top of batter with sugar.	ham and eggs

Chili Supper and Corn Muffins

1 lb. ground beef
½ cup chopped onion
2 tbsp. fat or drippings
1½ tsp. salt
½ tsp. pepper
½ tsp. chili powder (more if desired)
2 cups cooked tomatoes (no. 2 can)
2 cups cooked kidney beans (no. 2 can), drained

Brown beef and onion in fat in heavy skillet. Season with salt, pepper, and chili powder. Stir in tomatoes and kidney beans. Cover and simmer gently about 1 hr., stirring occasionally. Serve hot over Corn Muffins (recipe below). *6 servings*.

Corn Muffins: Heat oven to 450° (hot). Mix 1¼ cups Bisquick, ¾ cup corn meal, ½ tsp. salt, 2 tbsp. sugar, 1 egg, and ¾ cup milk and beat well with rotary beater. Fill greased medium muffin cups ⅔ full. Bake *15 to 20 min.* *Makes 12.*

Special Coffee Cakes

Apple Chip Brunch Cake

Heat oven to 400° (mod. hot). Add 2 tbsp. sugar, 2 tbsp. melted shortening to Coffee Cake (recipe page 8). Fold in 1 cup finely chopped pared apples. Spread in greased 9″ round layer pan, or 9″ square pan. Sprinkle with topping made by blending until crumbly, 2 tsp. cinnamon, ¼ cup sugar, 2 tbsp. Bisquick, and 2 tbsp. soft butter. Bake *20 to 25 min.*

Prune, Apricot, or Pineapple Coffee Cake

Heat oven to 400° (mod. hot). Make Coffee Cake (recipe page 8). Spread into greased 8″ round layer pan or 9″ square pan. Spread with 2 tbsp. butter, melted. Sprinkle with ¼ cup white or brown sugar (¾ tsp. cinnamon for prune topping). Arrange over top, 1 cup chopped, drained, cooked prunes or apricots or 1 cup drained crushed pineapple. Bake *20 to 25 min.*

133 Quicker Ways To Homemade, With Bisquick

Dumplings

Betty Crocker

Add ¾ cup milk to 2 cups Bisquick. Mix thoroughly with fork. Drop by spoonfuls onto chicken, meat, or vegetables in boiling stew (not into liquid). Cook over low heat for 10 minutes with kettle uncovered and 10 minutes with kettle covered. Liquid should just bubble gently. Remove dumplings. *Makes 10 to 12.*

Dress up your dumplings 5 ways

Kind	Add to recipe	Serve with
Corn	¾ cup whole kernel corn, 1 tbsp. chopped onion	beef stew
Walnut-Celery	½ cup coarsely chopped walnuts, ½ cup finely chopped celery	chicken fricassee
Raisin	½ cup raisins	chicken fricassee
Mint	½ tsp. dried mint	lamb stew
Pimiento-Green Pepper	2 tbsp. each chopped pimiento and green pepper	veal stew

Chicken Fricassee with Bisquick Dumplings

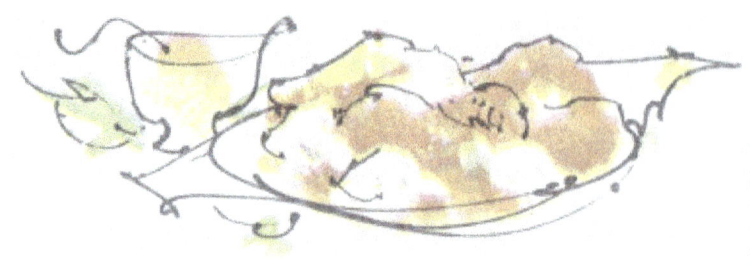

1 chicken (4 to 5 lb.) cut up
¼ cup fat
2 sprigs parsley
4 celery tops
1 carrot, sliced
1 slice of onion
2 tsp. salt
⅛ tsp. pepper

Brown chicken slowly in fat. Place in kettle with just enough boiling water to cover. Add rest of ingredients. Boil 5 min. Turn down heat and simmer until tender (2 to 3 hr.). Prepare and cook Dumplings (recipe page 10)—except add ¼ cup chopped parsley. Remove dumplings and chicken and place on platter. Keep hot while making Gravy (recipe below). *8 servings.*

Gravy: Leave chicken broth (about 4 cups) in kettle over low heat. Skim off excess fat. Mix ½ cup Bisquick and 1 cup milk or cold water to a smooth paste. Stir into broth. Cook until thickened (about 15 min.) stirring occasionally. Season to taste.

Sauerkraut with Franks and Dumplings

Add 2 cups water to two no. 303 cans sauerkraut in saucepan. Simmer 30 minutes. Bury 8 frankfurters (or 1 lb.) in sauerkraut. Prepare and cook ½ Dumplings (recipe page 10). Add ½ tsp. caraway seeds, if desired. Serve hot. *4 servings.*

Pork and Dumplings

Brown 6 pork chops in deep skillet or heavy kettle. Season. Add 1 medium onion, thinly sliced, and ¼ cup water. Cover skillet; simmer until meat is tender (40 to 50 min.). Add 1½ to 3 cups water. Prepare and cook Dumplings (recipe page 10). Remove meat and dumplings to hot platter while making gravy. *6 servings.*

Dessert Dumplings

Mix in saucepan 3 tbsp. Bisquick, 3 tbsp. sugar, and ¼ tsp. salt. Gradually stir in 1½ cups juice from canned fruit. Bring to boil; boil gently 2 min. stirring constantly. Stir in 1 cup canned or fresh fruit, 2 to 3 tsp. lemon juice, ½ tsp. grated lemon or orange rind, and $1/16$ tsp. nutmeg or cinnamon. Prepare and cook Dumplings (recipe page 10). Serve immediately. *6 servings.*

133 Quicker Ways To Homemade, With Bisquick

Nut Bread

Betty Crocker

½ cup sugar
1 egg
1¼ cups milk
3 cups Bisquick
1½ cups chopped Diamond Walnuts

Heat oven to 350° (mod.). Mix sugar, egg, milk, and Bisquick. Then beat vigorously for 30 seconds. Batter may still be slightly lumpy. Stir in Diamond Walnuts. Pour into well greased loaf pan, 9×5×3″. Bake *45 to 50 min.*, until toothpick stuck into center comes out clean. Crack in top is typical. Cool before slicing.

Banana Nut Bread

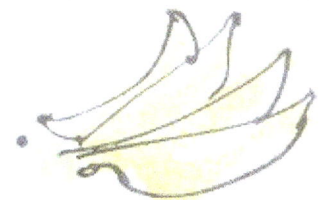

Follow Nut Bread recipe ([page 12](page_12))—except use ¾ cup sugar and only ½ cup milk. Use only ¾ cup chopped nuts and add 1 cup mashed bananas (2 to 3 bananas).

Orange Nut Bread

Follow Nut Bread recipe (page 12)—except use ¾ cup sugar and instead of milk use orange juice plus 1 tbsp. grated orange rind. Use only ¾ cup chopped nuts. Bake *50 to 55 min.*

Fruit Nut Bread

Follow Nut Bread recipe (page 12)—except use ¾ cup sugar and instead of milk use orange juice. Use only ¾ cup chopped nuts and add 1 cup chopped dried apricots or other dried fruit. Bake *55 to 60 min.*

Orange-Honey Nut Bread

Follow Nut Bread recipe (page 12)—except use only ¼ cup sugar and add ½ cup honey. Instead of 1¼ cups milk, use only ¾ cup orange juice plus 1 tbsp. grated orange rind. Use only ¾ cup chopped nuts.

Little Gift Breads

Bake them in cans! Follow Nut Bread recipe (page 12) or any of the variations. Divide batter between 3 well greased no. 2 cans or 5 well greased soup cans, filling cans slightly more than half full. Bake uncovered no. 2 cans *45 to 50 min.*; soup cans *about 40 min.* in *mod. oven* (350°) until toothpick stuck into center comes out clean.

Serving, Storing, Freezing Ideas:

• Cool thoroughly before slicing. Use thin sharp knife to prevent crumbling.

• Nut bread slices spread with cream cheese are delicious for teas as well as lunch boxes.

• Nut breads with the orange juice base are an excellent bread for mailing as a gift.

• Individual round nut breads make attractive gifts for Christmas and other holidays.

• Nut breads will keep a week in the refrigerator if wrapped tightly in aluminum foil, and will keep well wrapped in foil in the freezer.

Pancakes and Waffles

Waffles are topped with cherry jam, pancakes stacked with 1 cup warm chunk pineapple.

Pancakes: Add 1⅔ cups milk and 1 egg to 2 cups Bisquick. Beat with rotary beater until smooth. Grease griddle if necessary. Turn pancakes when bubbles appear. Between bakings, stir to thin out batter. *Makes about 18 pancakes.*

For thinner pancakes, use 2 cups milk.

Waffles: Follow Pancake recipe—except add 2 tbsp. cooking (salad) oil or melted shortening. Waffles are baked when they stop steaming. *Makes 2 large or 6 small.*

Note: Griddle or waffle iron is right temperature for baking when a few drops of water sprinkled on it jump around.

Dress up your pancakes or waffles 8 ways

Kind	Add to recipe	Serve with
Banana	1 cup mashed ripe bananas (2 med.), 1 tbsp. lemon juice, and 2 tbsp. sugar.	honey, currant jelly, or confectioners' sugar.
Blueberry	2 tbsp. sugar. Then fold in 1 cup fresh or drained canned blueberries.	honey or confectioners' sugar.
Corn	1 cup cream style or drained whole kernel corn with ½ tsp. paprika.	syrup, creamed dried beef or ham, or white sauce and bacon.
Cheese	½ to 1½ cups grated, sharp cheese.	syrup, creamed meats or vegetables.
Ham	1 to 1½ cups chopped cooked ham.	syrup, cranberry sauce, cheese sauce, creamed vegetables.
Nut	¾ to 1 cup finely chopped pecans, peanuts, or walnuts (toasted, if desired).	syrup, ice cream and caramel sauce.
Onion	1 to 1½ cups finely chopped onion, sautéed until golden brown in 2 or 3 tbsp. fat.	browned ground beef and gravy.

Spicy	1 tsp. cinnamon, ½ tsp. allspice, ½ tsp. cloves, and ½ tsp. nutmeg.	syrup or sweetened applesauce.

Chiffon Waffles: Follow recipe for Puff Pancakes (below) but use a waffle baker.

Chocolate Waffles: Make Waffles (recipe [page 14](page_14))—except add ½ cup sugar and 2 sq. unsweetened chocolate (2 oz.), melted, to batter.

Rich Pancakes: Make Pancakes (recipe [page 14](page_14))—except use 1¼ cups milk, 2 eggs, and 2 tbsp. cooking (salad) oil or melted shortening.

Puff Pancakes: Beat 2 eggs with rotary beater until soft peaks form. Blend in 1 cup milk. Add 2⅓ cups Bisquick and 2 tbsp. sugar. Mix just until thoroughly dampened. Fold in ¼ cup cooking (salad) oil or melted shortening. Spoon onto medium-hot ungreased griddle. When puffed up, and bubbles begin to break, cook on other side. Serve with syrup or as dessert with warm fruit, such as strawberries, and whipped cream. *Makes 15 to 20 pancakes.*

Main dish pancakes and waffles ...

Tuna Royal Pancakes

Pancakes (recipe page 14)
7-oz. can tuna, drained and broken
¼ cup chopped onion
½ cup grated Parmesan or processed cheese
½ cup chopped celery
¼ cup chopped pimiento
about 2 tsp. lemon juice
10½-oz. can cream of celery or chicken soup
2 tbsp. Bisquick
¼ tsp. salt
⅛ tsp. pepper
2 cups milk

Heat oven to 400° (mod. hot). Make 10 thinner pancakes (5″ size). Keep warm between towels until ready to serve. Mix tuna, onion, ¼ cup of the cheese, celery, pimiento, and lemon juice. Spoon 2 tbsp. of mixture on each pancake. Roll and place folded side down in 11½×7½×1½″ oblong baking dish. Heat in oven *about 10 min*. Mix soup, Bisquick, salt, pepper, and milk. Heat until thickened. Pour over pancakes and sprinkle with the remaining ¼ cup grated cheese. If desired, place under broiler until bubbly. *10 servings.*

Waffle Supper Royal

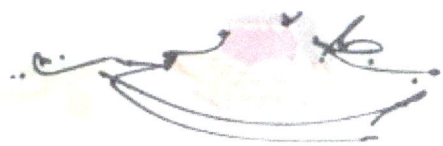

Serve waffles with creamed chicken or turkey and top with whole cranberry sauce. Wonderful Sunday supper!

Waffle Club Rabbit

Make Waffles (recipe page 14) using 2 cups milk. Bake until very crisp and brown. Serve waffles (whole or sections) with a slice or more of fresh tomato arranged on each serving. Spoon Cheese Sauce (recipe below) over, then top with strips of crisp bacon.

Cheese Sauce: Mix 1½ cups medium white sauce, 2 cups grated sharp Cheddar cheese (½ lb.). If desired, add ¼ tsp. dry mustard and few grains thyme. Heat slowly until cheese melts and blends with sauce. *6 servings.*

Chicken Griddle Cakes

Make 8 large Pancakes (recipe page 14) using about ½ cup batter for each. Spoon ¼ cup Creamed Chicken (recipe below) onto half of each pancake.

Fold over other half. Place on baking sheet. Sprinkle 1 tbsp. grated sharp cheese over each cake. Slip under broiler or in oven for a moment to melt cheese. *8 servings.*

Creamed Chicken: Melt 2 tbsp. butter. Remove from heat. Blend in ¼ cup Bisquick and 1 tsp. salt. Gradually stir in 1½ cups milk. Bring to boil over low heat, stirring constantly. Boil 1 min. Stir in 2 cups finely diced cooked chicken. Season to taste with pepper and poultry seasoning. Heat until chicken is hot.

Brunch and dessert pancakes

Sunday in Vermont Pancakes

Grate an apple into batter for Pancakes (recipe page 14). Make large pancakes 5″ across. Stack five high with warm cranberry sauce between layers. Sprinkle confectioners' sugar on top. Cut in wedges. Serve immediately.

Spiced Cherry Sauce for Pancakes

Mix ¾ cup sugar, 3 tbsp. cornstarch, ¼ tsp. cinnamon, and ⅛ tsp. salt in small saucepan. Add 1 cup chopped cherries (canned or fresh), 1 tbsp. lemon juice, and 1 cup water (or juice from canned cherries). Bring to boil over direct heat, stirring constantly. Boil 1 min. Serve hot. *Makes about 1½ cups sauce.*

Colonial Jelly Stack

Make Pancakes (recipe page 14). Use ½ cup batter for each pancake. Place 1 pancake on warm plate and while piping hot spread generously with soft butter and jelly. Top with second pancake. Spread and repeat until they are 6 high. Sprinkle top with confectioners' sugar. Cut stack into wedges. Serve hot. *6 servings.*

Maple Whip

Cream ½ cup *soft* butter. Add 1 cup maple-flavored syrup gradually. Beat until smooth and spreading consistency. Serve on hot pancakes or waffles. This can be refrigerated for future use.

Strawberry Blintzes

Pancakes (recipe page 14)
1 cup cottage cheese (small curd)
4-oz. pkg. cream cheese
1½ tbsp. lemon rind
3 tbsp. lemon juice
¼ cup sugar
10-oz. pkg. frozen strawberries (thawed)
1 tbsp. lemon juice
¼ tsp. almond extract

Heat oven to 400° (mod. hot). Combine cottage cheese, cream cheese, lemon rind, the 3 tbsp. lemon juice, and sugar; whip until creamy. Place ¼ cup filling on each pancake and roll up. Place rolled side down in 11×7" baking dish. Heat in oven for *10 min.* just before serving. Heat the strawberries, the 1 tbsp. lemon juice, and almond extract. Spoon over pancakes. Serve immediately. *6 servings.*

Quantity Pancakes

For 60 Pancakes. Serves 15.

10 cups Bisquick (40-oz. pkg. or two 20-oz. pkg.)
8⅓ cups milk
5 eggs

For 100 Pancakes. Serves 25.

15 cups Bisquick (60-oz. pkg.)
3 qt. milk
7 eggs

Add milk and eggs to Bisquick. Beat with rotary beater until smooth. Bake as directed on page 14.

Double-Decker Fruit Shortcake

Heat oven to 400° (mod. hot). Make Shortcake dough (recipe page 18) and roll into two 8″ square pieces. Fit one piece into an 8″ square pan, pressing dough about ½″ up sides of pan. Be careful to press together any tears in the dough. Spread 2 cups washed fresh raspberries or blueberries over dough, sprinkle with ¼ to ½ cup sugar. Cover with the other square of dough. Bake *about 25 min.*, until well browned. Cut into squares and serve warm or cold with Sauce (recipe below). *9 servings.*

Sauce: Mix ½ cup sugar and 1 tbsp. cornstarch in saucepan. Stir in ¼ cup cold water, ¼ cup butter, and 1 cup washed fresh raspberries or blueberries, mashed. Bring to a boil and boil 1 min.

Fruit Roll

Heat oven to 450° (hot). Measure ¾ cup sugar and ½ cup water into a 9″ square pan. Bring to a boil and boil 1 min. Make Shortcake dough (recipe page 18). Roll ¼" thick into an oblong, 15×7". Spread with 2 cups fresh fruit or well drained canned fruit. Sprinkle with ¼ cup sugar. Roll up beginning at wide side. Seal well by pinching edge of dough into roll. Cut into 9 slices about 1½" thick. Place slices cut-side-up in the pan of hot syrup. Bake *about 25 min.*, until golden brown. Serve warm with cream, if desired. *9 servings.*

Winter Shortcake

1 cup canned crushed pineapple (9-oz. can)
1 cup finely chopped or shredded red-skinned apple (1 med. to large apple)
1 cup finely chopped fresh cranberries (1 cup whole cranberries)
¼ cup sugar
⅛ tsp. salt

Mix all ingredients. Let stand at room temperature ½ to 1 hr. before serving. Make Shortcake dough (recipe page 18). Cut individual shortcakes. Split while piping hot and serve shortcake style with the fruit mixture. *6 servings.*

Peach-Orange Shortcake

Heat oven to 450° (hot). Make Shortcake dough (recipe page 18)—except add grated rind of 1 orange to Bisquick before adding liquid. Spread dough in greased 13×9½×2" pan. Sprinkle with 2 tbsp. sugar, if desired. Bake *10 to 12 min.* Cut into 12 squares. For each serving, spoon sliced peaches between 2 squares and on top. Top with whipped cream. *6 servings.*

Sour Cream-Strawberry Shortcake

Make Shortcake dough (recipe page 18). Cut individual shortcakes. Split layers. Spoon frozen strawberries and commercial sour cream between layers and over top.

Velvet Crumb Cake

1⅓ cups Bisquick
¾ cup sugar
3 tbsp. soft shortening
1 egg

¾ cup milk
1 tsp. vanilla

Heat oven to 350° (mod.). Grease and flour a square pan, 8×8×2″ or a round layer pan, 9×1½″. Mix Bisquick, sugar. Add shortening, egg, ¼ cup of milk. Beat vigorously 1 min. Stir in gradually remaining milk, vanilla. Beat ½ min. Pour into prepared pan. Bake *35 to 40 min.*

Broiled Toppings ...

While cake is warm spread on any one of these toppings and broil 3″ from heat.

Honey Crisp Topping: Cream until fluffy 3 tbsp. soft butter and ⅓ cup honey. Mix in thoroughly ¼ cup shredded coconut, ½ cup crushed Wheaties, and ½ cup drained crushed pineapple.

Broiled Orange Glaze: Mix 2 tbsp. soft butter, 3 tbsp. Bisquick, ¼ tsp. cinnamon, 2 tbsp. grated orange rind, and ¼ cup brown sugar (packed).

Broiled Peanut Butter Topping: Mix 2 tbsp. soft butter or other shortening, ⅓ cup brown sugar (packed), 2 tbsp. cream or top milk, ½ cup chopped peanuts, and 2 tbsp. peanut butter.

Other Toppings ...

Peach-Apricot Jam Topping: Spread ½ cup apricot or peach jam or preserves over the hot cake.

Streusel Topping: Mix with fork ¼ cup Bisquick, 2 tsp. cinnamon, 2 tbsp. brown sugar, and 1 tbsp. soft butter. Sprinkle on cake before baking.

Velvet Crumb Upside-down Cake

Melt over low heat 2 tbsp. butter in an 8" square pan. Sprinkle with ¼ cup brown sugar. Arrange fresh or well drained canned fruit over sugar. Make Velvet Crumb Cake (recipe page 20)—except pour batter over fruit in pan. Bake *35 to 40 min.* Invert pan at once on serving plate. Allow pan to remain over cake for a few minutes.

Orange-Nut Velvet Crumb Cake

Make Velvet Crumb Cake (recipe page 20)—except add ½ tsp. nutmeg, ½ tsp. orange extract, ½ cup seedless raisins or currants, ¼ cup chopped nuts, and 2 tbsp. grated orange rind with the shortening. Bake *about 30 min.* Serve warm with whipped cream.

Velvet Fudge Cake

Make Velvet Crumb Cake (recipe page 20)—except add ⅓ cup cocoa to the Bisquick. Pour half of batter into prepared pan. Spread with half of Chocolate Coconut Topping (recipe below). Pour remaining batter into pan. Bake *35 to 40 min*. Immediately spread with rest of topping. Serve warm.

Chocolate-Coconut Topping: Mix ½ cup (½ pkg.) semi-sweet chocolate pieces, melted, ⅓ cup water, 2 cups finely chopped coconut.

Velvet Crumb Spice Cake

Make Velvet Crumb Cake (recipe page 20)—except use ¾ cup brown sugar (packed) in place of white. Add ½ tsp. cinnamon, ¼ tsp. *each* cloves, allspice, and nutmeg with Bisquick. Bake *about 30 min*. Serve warm with a topping.

Velvet Crumb Shortcake

Make Velvet Crumb Cake (recipe page 20). Cut cake into 6 to 9 pieces while still warm. Spoon sweetened sliced strawberries between split pieces and on top.

Yeast Baking

Hurry-up Yeast Rolls

1. Dissolve 1 pkg. active dry yeast in ¾ cup warm water (not hot—105° to 115°). Mix in 2½ cups Bisquick. Beat vigorously.

2. Turn dough onto surface well dusted with Bisquick. Knead until smooth, about 20 times.

3. Shape into 12 pan rolls. Place in greased 8″ round layer pan.

4. Place pan of rolls on wire rack over a bowl of hot water and cover with towel; let rise about 1 hr.

Heat oven to 400° (mod. hot). Bake *10 to 15 min.*, until a rich golden brown. Brush with butter after baking. Serve hot. *Makes 16.*

1. Water temperature for dissolving yeast is right when it is slightly warmer than lukewarm. Too hot water kills the yeast; too cool water retards rising.

2. Rolls are ready to bake when dough is puffy and light and slight indentation remains in dough when pressed gently with finger.

Variations in Shapes

Crescent Rolls

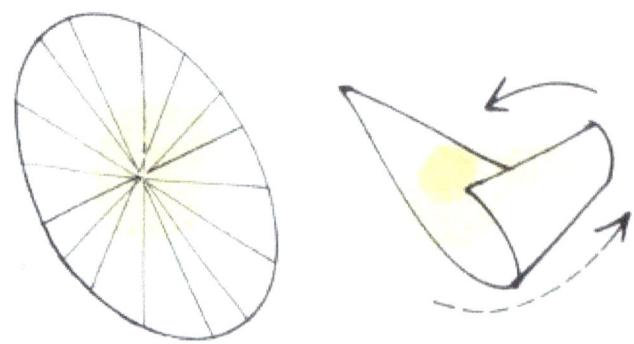

Roll dough into 12″ circle. Cut into 16 wedges. Beginning at wide side roll toward point. Place on greased baking sheet with point underneath.

Clothespin Rolls

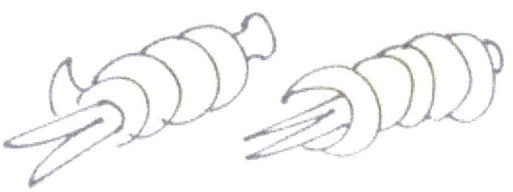

Divide dough into 16 to 18 strips. Roll each on board with palms of hands into 12″ lengths. Wrap strips around greased clothespins so edges barely touch.

Knots

Make strips (as above). Twist and tie each strip into a knot. Press ends down on greased baking sheet.

More yeast bakings

Pizza

(Makes four 10" Pizzas)

Follow directions for Yeast dough (recipe page 23) through the kneading. Divide dough into 4 pieces. Roll each piece paper-thin into a circle, about 10" in diameter. Place on ungreased baking sheets or in shallow pie pans. No rising! Top with:

¾ cup chopped onion
1 clove garlic, chopped
2 cups tomato sauce
1 cup chopped salami or cooked Italian sausage or 2 cans anchovies, chopped
salt and pepper to taste
2½ cups grated Mozzarella cheese or two 6-oz. pkg. sliced Mozzarella cheese (cut into thin strips)

Mix onion, garlic, tomato sauce, salami, salt, and pepper and spread on dough. Sprinkle grated cheese over all or lay cheese strips on top. Sprinkle with oregano to desired taste. *Heat oven to 425° (hot). Bake 15 to 20 min.*, until crust is brown and filling hot and bubbly. Serve immediately. Unbaked pizza may stand while others are baking.

Individual Pizzas

Divide dough into 8 pieces and roll each piece into 5" circles. Spread with filling and bake.

Easy Pizzas

Divide dough in half and roll each part on a baking sheet as thin as desired. Spread with filling.

Italian Bread Sticks

Follow directions for Yeast dough (recipe page 23). Divide dough into 16 equal parts. Roll each piece between hands into pencil-like strips 8″ long. Melt ¼ cup butter. Spread part of butter in bottom of 13×9½×2″ oblong pan. Put strips of dough in pan. Brush tops with rest of butter. Sprinkle with caraway seeds, poppy seeds, celery seeds, sesame seeds, or garlic salt. Cover with damp cloth. Let rise in warm place (85°) until light, about 1 hr. *Heat oven to 425°* (hot). Bake *15 min.*, until light golden brown. Turn oven off. Allow bread sticks to remain in oven 15 more minutes to crisp.

Bisquick Herb Yeast Rolls

Follow directions for Yeast dough (recipe page 23)—except add ¼ tsp. nutmeg, ½ tsp. sage, and 1 tsp. caraway seeds to the Bisquick.

Mustard Buns for Hot Dogs

Follow directions for Yeast dough (recipe page 23)—except add 2 level tbsp. prepared mustard. Divide dough into 8 pieces; shape like a hot dog bun.

Onion Buns

Follow directions for Yeast dough (recipe page 23)—except add ½ cup finely chopped onion and use 2⅔ cups Bisquick. Divide dough into 10 portions and shape in oblongs or rounds. Good with wieners and hamburgers.

Hawaiian Yeast Rolls

¾ cup drained crushed pineapple
½ cup brown sugar (packed)
¼ cup soft butter
½ cup warm water (not hot—105 to 115°)
1 pkg. active dry yeast
1 egg
1 tbsp. granulated sugar
2½ cups Bisquick
2 tbsp. butter
¼ cup brown sugar (packed)

Mix pineapple, ½ cup brown sugar, and ¼ cup butter. Divide among 12 large greased muffin cups. Prepare dough by dissolving yeast in water. Mix in egg, 1 tbsp. sugar, and Bisquick; beat vigorously. Turn dough onto surface well dusted with Bisquick. Knead until smooth, about 20 times. Roll into a rectangle, 16×9″. Spread with rest of ingredients. Roll up tightly beginning at wide side. Seal well by pinching edge of dough into roll. Slice into 12. Place in prepared muffin cups. Place pan of rolls on wire rack over bowl of hot water and cover with towel; let rise 1 hr. *Heat oven to 400°* (mod. hot). Bake *15 min.* Invert pan; serve.

Caramel Buns

¼ cup soft butter
⅓ cup brown sugar (packed)
1 tsp. light corn syrup
⅓ cup pecans or walnuts
¾ cup warm water (not hot—105 to 115°)
1 pkg. active dry yeast
2½ cups Bisquick
2 tbsp. soft butter
¼ cup brown sugar (packed)
1 tsp. cinnamon

Melt butter; add brown sugar and corn syrup. Bring syrup mixture to a rolling boil. Spread in 8″ round layer pan. Add pecans. Dissolve yeast in warm water. Mix in Bisquick and beat vigorously. Turn dough onto surface well dusted with Bisquick. Knead until smooth, about 20 times. Roll out into rectangle, 16×9″. Spread with butter, sugar, and cinnamon. Roll up tightly beginning at wide side. Seal well by pinching edge of dough into roll. Slice into 10 slices. Place in pan. Place pan of rolls on wire rack over bowl of hot water and cover with towel; let rise 1 hr. *Heat oven to 400°* (mod. hot). Bake *20 to 25 min.* Invert pan and serve rolls warm.

Orange Rolls

Follow recipe for Hawaiian Yeast Rolls (above)—except substitute ½ cup orange juice, ½ cup sugar, and 2 tbsp. grated orange rind for the first two ingredients. Mix the orange juice, ½ cup sugar, orange rind, and ¼ cup butter in saucepan. Cook 2 min. over low heat. Divide among 12 muffin cups.

More Bisquick favorites

Berry Chiffon Short Pie

¼ cup sugar
1 envelope unflavored gelatin (1 tbsp.)
10-oz. pkg. frozen raspberries or strawberries, thawed
3 egg whites
¼ tsp. cream of tartar
⅓ cup sugar
½ cup whipping cream, whipped

Blend in saucepan sugar, gelatin, raspberries. Bring to full rolling boil, stirring constantly. Cool pan in cold water until mixture mounds slightly when dropped from a spoon. Add cream of tartar to egg whites, beat until frothy. Gradually beat in sugar and beat until meringue holds stiff peaks. Fold berry mixture into meringue. Carefully fold in whipped cream. Pile into cooled baked Short Pie shell (recipe below). Chill several hours until set.

Short Pie Shell

1 cup Bisquick
¼ cup soft butter (½ stick)
3 tbsp. boiling water

Heat oven to 450° (hot). Put Bisquick and butter in 9" pie pan. Add boiling water and stir vigorously with fork until dough forms a ball and cleans the pan. Dough will be puffy and soft. With fingers and heel of hand, pat dough evenly into pie pan, bringing up dough to edge of pan. This may seem skimpy but will not be when baked. Flute edges. Bake *8 to 10 min.* Fill with ice cream or other fillings.

Fruit Cobbler

Heat oven to 400° (mod. hot). Heat 2½ cups (no. 2 can) canned fruit or berries and juice (or 3 cups fresh fruit and ¾ cup water). Sweeten to taste. Blend in 1 tbsp. cornstarch dissolved in 2 tbsp. cold water. Bring to a boil; boil 1 min. Pour into 2-qt. baking dish. Dot with butter. Sprinkle with cinnamon. Drop ½ Fruit Shortcake Dough (recipe [page 18](page_18)) by spoonfuls over top. Bake about *20 min.* Serve hot with cream. *6 to 8 servings.*

Short Pie Rounds

Prepare Short Pie dough (above)—except divide dough into 6 parts. Flatten each part into 3 or 4" rounds on baking sheet. Flute edges. Bake *about 8 min.* Serve on top of your favorite cooked fruit filling. *6 servings.*

Ranch Pudding

    1 cup brown sugar (packed)
    2½ cups water
    2 tbsp. butter
    1 cup brown sugar (packed)
    ½ cup milk
    1¼ cups Bisquick
    1 cup raisins or chopped dates
    ½ to 1 cup chopped nuts
    1 tsp. vanilla

Heat oven to 350° (mod.). Mix 1 cup brown sugar, water, and butter in saucepan. Boil 5 min. Pour into 8" square pan. Mix rest of ingredients in bowl. Spoon batter on top of sugar mixture. It will sink into the liquid and will spread out as it bakes. Bake *45 min.* Serve warm with plain or whipped cream. *9 servings.*

Hot Sea Food Appetizers

Heat oven to 450° (hot). Make Rolled Biscuit dough (recipe page 3). Roll dough ¼" thick. Cut into biscuits 1" in diameter. Place on baking sheet. Bake *6 to 8 min.* Immediately split each baked biscuit. Spread with sea food mixture. Sprinkle with grated sharp cheese, if desired. Replace tops. Return to oven to heat through. Serve piping hot. *Makes about 60 tiny* biscuits.

Filling variations

Shrimp Spread: Mix ½ cup flaked cooked shrimp (5-oz. can), 1 tbsp. chopped pimiento, 1 tbsp. lemon juice, 3 tbsp. mayonnaise, and salt and pepper to taste.

Crabmeat Spread: Use crabmeat in place of shrimp in the above spread.

Pronto Puppies

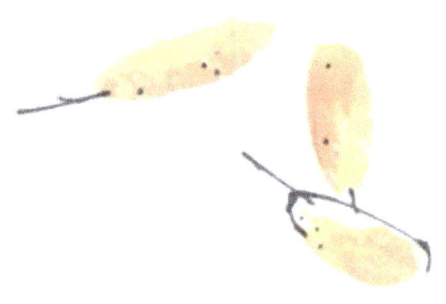

1 egg
½ cup milk
1 cup Bisquick
2 tbsp. yellow corn meal
¼ tsp. paprika
½ tsp. dry mustard
⅛ tsp. cayenne
1 lb. miniature or large frankfurters

Heat deep fat to 375°. Blend egg, milk. Stir in dry ingredients. Dip frankfurters in batter. Fry until brown, *2 to 3 min.* on each side. Serve miniature franks on cocktail picks. Slice large franks. To reheat: Place in 400° oven about 5 min.

www.ingramcontent.com/pod-product-compliance
Lightning Source LLC
Chambersburg PA
CBHW081628100526
44590CB00021B/3650